ISBN 978-1-5281-3478-1
PIBN 10918110

1 MONTH OF
FREE
READING

at

www.ForgottenBooks.com

By purchasing this book you are eligible for one month membership to ForgottenBooks.com, giving you unlimited access to our entire collection of over 1,000,000 titles via our web site and mobile apps.

To claim your free month visit: www.forgottenbooks.com/free918110

English
Français
Deutsche
Italiano
Español
Português

www.forgottenbooks.com

Mythology Photography **Fiction**
Fishing Christianity **Art** Cooking
Essays Buddhism Freemasonry
Medicine **Biology** Music **Ancient
Egypt** Evolution Carpentry Physics
Dance Geology **Mathematics** Fitness
Shakespeare **Folklore** Yoga Marketing
Confidence Immortality Biographies
Poetry **Psychology** Witchcraft
Electronics Chemistry History **Law**
Accounting **Philosophy** Anthropology
Alchemy Drama Quantum Mechanics
Atheism Sexual Health **Ancient History**
Entrepreneurship Languages Sport
Paleontology Needlework Islam
Metaphysics Investment Archaeology
Parenting Statistics Criminology
Motivational

THE UNIVERSITY OF NORTH CAROLINA LIBRARY EXTENSION PUBLICATION

VOL. XI | MAY, 1946 | NO. 6

WOMEN AND THE WIDE WORLD

Elizabeth Chesley Baity

Published six times a year, October, January, April, May, June, and July, by the University of North Carolina Press. Entered as second-class matter February 5, 1926, under the act of August 24, 1912. Chapel Hill, N. C.

CONTENTS

TABLE OF CONTENTS (Continued)

TABLE OF CONTENTS (Continued)

INTRODUCTION

It is obvious that the chapters in this course of study are in reverse order. Everyone knows that before an individual can try to set the outside world straight, he must put his inner world in order. "Neither death, exile, pain, nor anything of this kind is the real cause of our doing or not doing any action, but our inward opinions and principles." Nothing much has occurred in nearly twenty centuries to make this any less true than it was in the time of Epictetus. It is still the ideas we have inside that we translate into action in the community, the nation, the world.

Logically, therefore, our course should begin with chapter XII, which deals with the creation of a free human spirit, and end with a chapter I, a study of the international machinery necessary to create a society fit for free human spirits.

The trouble is, we don't have TIME to perfect ourselves before turning to the problem of world peace. If Willy is drowning, you don't pull out his feet and dry them off before getting his head out of the water. Dry feet are of no use to dead Willy. Sincere if somewhat short-sighted people insist that until we cure our problems at home, we've no business trying to cure those of the world. Let us treat this advice as the disguised defeatism which it is.

In the day of the jet-propelled robot plane and the atomic bomb, the whole world *is* the home of the modern woman and her family. The sooner we all learn this, the safer that world will be for everyone. It would be tidy if we could finish up our domestic problems before tackling the difficult job of world organization. Tidy—but time forbids. We must put the most urgent matter first even at the cost of temporarily slighting less pressing duties; sane people do not quibble over minutiae in the face of impending disaster. No one generation can hope to solve the problems of the world. Our own, however, faces catastrophe unless we relieve inter-national stresses caused by short-sighted self-interest. It is our task to rise above the obvious difficulties and to create a world government strong enough to prevent a third and inconceivably destructive world war. Let us get it entirely clear that no personal duty we owe our families is more important to their future than this one. It is every man's job and every woman's.

In the second part of this course we will survey certain indications that our democracy is not yet perfect, that justice does not always sweetly prevail, and that there is slightly more than a suspicion of disorder and inefficiency on the home front. After sifting the evidence offered by the books on psychology, we may grant that our society is imperfect partly because we ourselves are as full of flaws as a net is full of holes. But a net, though it does not keep off the rain, serves effectively to catch fish; our job is to work with what we have, where we are.

The last part of this course is the study of personal relations in marriage, child-care, and in the community. Here again we find that the survival of outmoded attitudes and institutions brings about unnecessary fear and anxiety, feelings of injustice and resentment, and other conditions that frustrate personality. We find again, too, that the best answer given us by psychiatrists takes us back again to the matter of our own inward opinions and attitudes. After two thousand years, we still fail to catch the points made repeatedly by Christ: that each individual must use his own talent, instead of burying it, that it is the beam in our own eye rather than the mote in our neighbor's that interferes with our vision, and that the better life we want must begin within our own hearts.

We will need all our resources to meet the necessities of life in the Atomic Age. The books used in this course give many suggestions for increasing the effectiveness of individuals and groups. They list state and national organizations already in the various fields of service. Books alone can never solve problems but they can analyze them and point the way for individual and group activity.

To know which are the most important of our problems is vastly more urgent today than it was when Lincoln said: " If we could first know where we are and whither we are tending, we could better judge what to do and how to do it." And so we turn to what is beyond any doubt the first of our problems: the creation of a world government to replace the international anarchy of the sovereign nations.

CHAPTER I

THE PRICE OF PEACE

"Meanwhile, the solution is to keep on writing, to sit down once a day, to address a new envelope with a great name, to rephrase the great hope and to demand action."—The Great Union

When the first atomic bomb fell much more went up in smoke than one Japanese city. The "security" of powerful armies and navies, national wealth and skill, of friendly neighboring nations, of leagues and alliances, of oceans and distance, vanished at once into thin air. There was smoke-writing on the sky above Hiroshima. Transcribed by the American scientists who produced the atomic bomb, the message read: no nation, however powerful, can put a fence around the explosive mixture of brains, uranium and hate; no defense, however skilful, exists against the "one-day war" of tomorrow's jet-propelled-robot-atomic-bomb.

Even we lucky Americans have one chance only to live out our lives free from the threat of sudden destruction. That chance is the speedy creation of a world government capable of solving the problems that lead to war. But what peace-plan can resolve the determination of many nations to expand their boundary lines at every possible point and to give up none of their sovereignty?

Upon the heartbreaking muddle of this international anarchy Emery Reves plays the searchlight of an exceptionally well-trained and creative mind in a book which makes the problems of peace clearer perhaps than some patriots would like to see them made.

Studying all the wars of history, Mr. Reves isolated one always present factor: the existence of two or more sovereign units. Peace, he found, existed only when the sovereign units were merged into a greater unit, capable of making law and enforcing it. "We are living in complete anarchy," says Mr. Reves, "because in a small world, interrelated in every other respect, there are seventy or eighty separate sources of law—seventy or eighty sovereignties." In short, the "sovereign nation" is no longer suited to the realities of life, and the price we pay for it is the possibility of destruction.

In *Foreign Policy Begins at Home*, James P. Warburg says that although we all want a just peace, we are inclined to leave it to the experts. Every citizen, says Mr. Warburg, has a responsibility in these matters which he must exercise. His book tells how the individual can further the cause of peace by his own conviction and behavior, since the sum total of our individual personal beliefs makes our belief as a nation, which in turn expresses itself in our foreign policy.

In *The United Nations Primer*, Sigrid Arne gives the background of the organization that, however inadequate at present, is our most immediate hope of peace. Newspapers and radio will make clear the difficulties facing the United Nations.

Many thoughtful people believe war can never be prevented by this power-alliance plan, but only by a world federation with a constitution like that of our United States. *The Great Nation* gives a blue-print for such a federation. David Cort, reminding us that the people of the United States constitute the real sovereignty of our nation, agrees with Mr. Reves that our most urgent duty is to use that sovereignty to build an effective world government.

1. CAUSES OF WAR

The Anatomy of Peace, by Emery Reves

Discuss: the author, his background; the growth of Nationalism in the past two centuries. Show why industrialism and nationalism inevitably breed authoritarian governments, and how the conflict between outmoded political institutions and the realities of the modern world produce war. The road to Fascism: "the vehicle is nationalism; the terminus is totalitarianism."

Analyze carefully the author's argument that the real cause of modern war is the conflict between industrialism, nationalism, and the interdependence of the modern world, and that the only possible cure is a world government based on laws and capable of enforcing them: "Human freedom is created by law and can exist only within a legal order, never without or beyond."

2. PEACE BY PATCHWORK?

Foreign Policy Begins at Home, by James B. Warburg
America's Place in the World, by Nathaniel Peffer

European Manifesto, by Pierre de Lanux

Can we leave a just peace to the "experts?" Sum up Mr. Warburg's analysis of fascism, "the gang against the people," and of American "hand-maidens of fascism." How has our foreign policy reflected our domestic policy? Have we been "isolated?" Discuss: "America is a party to every major war"; the annihilation of distance; how it happened that "our whole economic power was put behind Japan before the China-Japan war" (Peffer 67); why the League failed—"nobody of final consequence in world politics believed in it." America's choice—the way of power, Anglo-American Alliance, or World State? Discuss the drastic re-allocation of income from social betterment, public health, housing, etc., that would be necessary for a unilateral "bigstick" policy.

Explain: "Americans must cease to be ignorant," "There must be an end to amateurishness," "More Americans must make a career of certain countries and regions." (Peffer, 169 to 170)

Sum up Mr. Warburg's "what we can do."

European Manifesto. Give the comment of Pierre de Lanux on how the will of the majority of Americans in favor of the World Court was defeated in 1935; on American opinion and neutrality legislation; American sympathy for China and supplies for Japan; the four American attitudes—isolation, "bigstick power, collaboration, and accepted solidarity with democratic nations."

Discuss current United States world plans: how can individuals support constructive American leadership in foreign affairs? Why must we encourage a United Europe?

3. UNITED STATES OF THE WORLD?

United Nations Primer, by Sigrid Arne

Trace briefly the basic points of the chief international agreements that preceded the San Francisco Conference. What were the chief areas of disagreement among the powers? Why does Russia fear that we will help rebuild Germany?

Discuss the following: The Food Conference: what changes could be made in food production and distribution? The UNRRA: the scope of its work, how the funds are to be spent, the problems of "displaced persons." Bretton Woods: what is the function of the Fund and of the Bank?

The Five Freedoms: how effectively are we achieving them?

Summarize the chief accomplishments of the San Francisco Conference.

The Great Union, by David Cort

Discuss the parallel between the present and 1789. Compare the United Nations agreement with the Articles of the Confederacy. Many people advocate a federal union. What forces oppose it? Compare the "illustrative constitution" for the Great Union with our United States Constitution and Bill of Rights. What methods can we use to bring about an effective world organization? Is your club taking steps to let your representatives know what you expect of them in this attempt?

Additional Reading:

    The Time for Decision, by Sumner Welles. Especially valuable for its discussion of the problem of German aggression, and its plan for a world organization based upon regional systems.

    The Making of Tomorrow, by Raoul de Roussy de Sales, analyzes brilliantly the dangers of nationalism, collectivism, and pacifism.

    A *Preface to Peace,* by Harold Callender, is a journalist's account of events that led to World War II, and of the need for a constructive, creative world union.

CHAPTER II

OUR ENEMIES SPEAK FOR THEMSELVES

"I have often felt a bitter pang at the thought of the German people, so estimable as individuals, so wretched in the whole."
—Goethe

The authors listed below go thoroughly into the problem of the causes of the war which has cost the world so many millions dead, so many more millions wrecked for life. Although we admit our own failure to play a decisive role in shaping events after World War I, the fact remains that World War II was caused by specific nations who planned it, prepared for it, and began it by destroying their weakest neighbors first. How may we prevent a third and infinitely more destructive world war from arising from these same sources?

The authors of *Europe Free and United* and *European Manifesto* say that only a knowledge of how the German mind works, and what German purposes are, can enable us to deal with Germany in a way that may delay or prevent the outbreak of another world war. Ludwig, Sayers and Kahn show, through quotations from German leaders, how German thought and action for the past century has been directed towards the destruction of western civilization. They trace the steps by which the German General Staff, spearhead of the Prussian Junker class, aided by German industrialists, crushed all Christian and democratic ideas and molded German thought into a pattern of ruthless inhuman aggression. These writers show that it is futile to hope to find in present-day Germany elements upon which to build a democracy, that Hitler and the Nazi party were the flowering of sinister seeds long germinating in the German soul.

They offer evidence that to the real rulers of Germany the Nazis were merely a means to an end, a tool now discarded just as the monarchy was discarded after World War I. The world must realize, they emphasize, that this ruling core in Germany, though now gone underground, is still determined upon conquest by whatever diabolical means can be acquired, and entirely capable of developing those means if permitted to do so.

Otto Tolischus has given a similar record with regard to the "honorable Aryans" by means of quotations that reflect Japanese determination on world conquest. The master-race concept is hereditary with the Japanese, says Mr. Tolischus, and has been strengthened by a state-organized religion deliberately employing the treachery and savagery of the jungle age. This compilation shows how mistaken it would be to assume that Japanese hopes went up in smoke at Hiroshima, since defeat in 1945 is only an unfortunate but minor phase of their "glorious Hundred Year War." As Japanese leaders put it, "History teaches us that such great tasks take at least one or two centuries to accomplish."

If history and these records teach anything to us, the Americans, it must be that we dare not sit back and consider victory won. The only lasting conquest of an aggressor nation lies in the re-education of the people, but this is a slow process difficult to accomplish from the outside. We must strike directly at the root of conflict, at the existence of sovereign nations equipped for war and answerable to no higher power. This can be done only by creating a system of law to which the nations will be answerable.

Our men of science have been clever enough to reorient the molecules in an atom. A strange obituary notice will be in order if our men of government are not clear-sighted enough to reorient man-made concepts in time to prevent our destruction as a consequence of our own cleverness.

1. PAN-GERMANISM AND ITS PLAN

The Moral Conquest of Germany, by Emil Ludwig

European Manifesto, by Pierre de Lanux

> Discuss: the influence of the Junker class on German thought; German conquests of the past century; the work of the German General Staff following World War I, its plans for World War III, and its current propaganda aims; the methods of total war.
>
> Analyze the German character: its craving for power and inability to understand fair play and democracy; its contempt for women and the lower classes.
>
> Discuss the German attitude towards the Jews, and the German refusal to admit war guilt.

The Plot Against the Peace, by Michael Sayers and Albert Kahn

Discuss: the secret history of Nazism, the German General Staff's plan of world conquest, the army of murderers, the policy of genocide, the Fehme in Germany and in America. Discuss the plan of camouflaged capital, the conversion of the Nazi party into an underground, and the planned organization of sympathy in the United States.

Name the organizations in America for Fascist propaganda during the war. What elements prevented the conviction of the leaders of these movements?

2. JAPANESE BLUEPRINT FOR CONQUEST

Through Japanese Eyes, by Otto D. Tolischus

Discuss, giving the words of the Japanese themselves, the following: the master-race and its God-Emperor of the world; plan for world conquest; "blood and iron" rule; "We must first crush the United States."

The methods: the Japanese one-party system, with its destruction of individualism and its opposition to labor unions and liberal thought; the use of anti-semitism to create discord among the Allies; the principles of Japanese diplomacy: "The divine mission of Japan puts her above treaty-breaking because what would be wrong in the rest of the world is right in Japan." Trace briefly our diplomatic history with Japan up to Pearl Harbor.

Summarize the Japanese view on Americans, the prophecy of our disintegration and collapse, how the Japanese planned to overthrow the English and the Americans. Prelude in China: the Japanese invasion of China and the plans for domination of Asia.

3. OUR ENEMIES AND THE FUTURE

References as above

Europe Free and United, by Albert Guerard

Use current news-magazines to bring this discussion up to date

Analyze briefly, from current news sources, the post-war attitude of the Germans and the Japanese: have they a sense of war guilt? What type of governments do they seem to support? Compare, if possible, their war losses in population and national wealth with those of their neighbors. Compared with surrounding countries, has Germany "lost" World War II?

Discuss in detail the suggestions given in these books for the treatment of the Germans: destruction of the war machine; over-throw of the power of Prussia; German responsibility for the restoration of destroyed territories; post-war "occupation."

The issue: world anarchy or world republic? Compare the discussions given by de Lanux and Guerard for a European Commonwealth. Can England, the Soviet Union, and Germany form a workable commonwealth? Discuss: is the United States helping to create world union, or do we again support peace-by-patchwork?

The solution: what does de Lanux mean by "false realism and false efficiency?" (118); by "What we need . . . is a full civic education, and more faith in ourselves . . ."; by the need for "revolution within man himself?"

Additional Reading:

The Coming Struggle for Peace, by André Visson. This book, a detailed study of the claims of the various European countries, shows how hopeless the problems of peace are when viewed from the vantage-point of national interests.

Main Street's New Neighbors, by Melvin K. Whiteleather

CHAPTER III

UNDERSTANDING OUR ALLIES: RUSSIA AND CHINA

"It was the Russian workers whom the enemy perhaps under-estimated more than Russian soldiers."—Edgar Snow

The books to be reviewed in the next two chapters, for all their difference in subject-matter and viewpoint, make one thing very clear: that we Americans have no consistent, dependable foreign policy. What is the cause of this American myopia? One cause, as the following books indicate, is that instead of looking directly at the country and the people with whom we must deal, we consult a set of pre-conceived labels. Instead of seeing people, we see "capitalists," "communists," "imperialists," "socialists," etc. But reality defies such over-simplified classifications. Studying facts instead of labels, we observe Soviet Russia behaving in foreign affairs like an imperial nation; England, mother-country of capitalistic imperialism, voting herself into domestic socialism; the United States, alleged home of democratic liberalism, displaying reactionary trends which unhappily may be read by him who runs for office.

Edgar Snow and Richard Lauterbach, making off-the-record contacts in Russia, found that the American picture of Russia differs from the reality in many ways. They show why most Russians are willing to make present sacrifices for an economic and political system that Americans would find restrictive, and ask that we try to understand how much more World War II cost the Russians than it cost us. When Hitler sent his forces eastward their instructions were clear enough: "Twenty million people must be wiped out. From now on, this will be one of the principal aims of German policy." Many millions of Russians died in unspeakable ways, areas of Russia almost as large as our own country were devastated, and these sacrifices and achievements seem to the Russians to have given them the right to make certain decisions to insure that this will not happen again.

But what have ordinary Americans to do with foreign policy, we may wonder? The following observers make the point that though our foreign representatives should have a much greater degree of understanding of the country and the people with whom they deal, this is not enough. We at home, who in the long run affect foreign policy by our approval or disapproval of it, must quit thinking in labels. We must learn more about the psychology and the problems of the people of other countries.

Before the Japanese returned our scrap iron to us with compound interest at Hawaii they tested their equipment and savagery on the Chinese, who stood between them and the resources of Asia. *People on Our Side* is a record of those heroic years when China fought alone, receiving no help from anyone and facing an enemy buying material from the United States and the British Empire as well as from her Axis Allies.

Mr. Rowe, summing up China's post-war potentialities in *China Among the Powers*, believes that China can develop the strength needed to play a strong role in Asia only if the Allies aid her. But will Anglo-American and Soviet policies combine to strengthen China? And if so—which China?

Edgar Snow and Harrison Forman, two of the few white men familiar with the Border Region called "Communist China," tell us something about the people who number three-fourths of our United States population. Unquestionably they resisted the Japanese bravely with inadequate homemade weapons. The Japanese feared them, Mr. Forman wrote, because they were volunteer fighters with principles, and because they had "achieved a miracle in China—the respect and cooperation of the people."

1. THE WHY OF RUSSIA'S MONROE DOCTRINE

These Are the Russians, by Richard E. Lauterbach
The Pattern of Soviet Power, by Edgar Snow

> The war: Leningrad and Sevastopol. The Rumanians and the Germans in Russia; "Murder, incorporated." Russian war costs. Tell how the Russians are rebuilding. Discuss punishment for racial discrimination; scientific training for all young people. Russia's verdict on Germany: retraining of Nazi prisoners.
>
> Russian life today: read, "I know this place must not seem very grand to you, coming from America, but compared to old Russia it is a heaven above hell." (Snow, p. 114) Discuss: why socialism is working in Russia. Explain: "the Russians save their indoctrination efforts for their own people;" the new Russian marriage laws; the swing towards tradition in architecture, religion, and social customs.

Science in Russia: "restoring the clinical dead"; transparent steel; a wheat to abolish famine; the broad scientific education of Russian youth.

Stalin and his assistants; Soviet system of local committees; the men from whom tomorrow's leader will be chosen: their work habits, and their lack of personal wealth. How do Soviet officials know what the people are thinking?

Discuss Stalin's question: "How much will we have to buy to keep all your people employed?" (Lauterbach, 120)

2. CHINA AND HER PROBLEMS

China Among the Powers, by David Nelson Rowe

China After Seven Years of War, by Hollington K. Tong

"We have no Foreign Policy—Why?" by John Coriden Lyons, in *The South and World Affairs*

The Chinese people: village life, student life, women in journalism, industry, law and government. What factors make the Chinese progress towards constitutional government difficult?

Discuss: over-population, malnutrition and lack of public health services.

Review: Chinese courage in the Burma Jungles; American aid to the Chinese; Red China's opposition to Japan.

China and the future of Asia: her resources for military power—manpower, agriculture, and industrial raw materials; the chief problems of her industrial development, of transport and communications, of government and social organization.

Explain what Mr. Lyons means by questioning American "solutions" for Chinese problems.

3. BACKGROUND TO CIVIL WAR

Report from Red China, by Harrison Forman

Patterns of Soviet Power, by Edgar Snow

Current Periodicals

Politics of the Border Region: discuss the platform of the Chinese Communists; the liberation of the "slaves" of Chinese Feudalism, co-operative agriculture and industry, universal education, government by regional committees.

Life in Red China: converting loafers to labor heroes, medicine versus witchcraft, Yenan University married women students, village democracy.

Discuss China's 80 percent rural population. What plans have the Nationalists for these people? What does Mao Tse-tung advocate? Give brief character sketches of the leaders of Red China.

Red China against the Japanese: summarize the military actions of the Eighth Route Army; discuss anti-Japanese bases, mine fighters, women warriors.

Why does Chiang oppose the Kungchantang? Read the Atkinson quotation on why Chiang and Stilwell could not get along. Explain the vital importance of who controls Manchuria.

CHAPTER IV

OLD FRIENDS AND NEW GOOD NEIGHBORS

"These two great organizations of the English-speaking democracies, the British Empire and the United States, will have to be somewhat mixed up together in some of their affairs for mutual and general advantage."—Winston Churchill

Though the English and the Americans have been sniping at each other ever since the days of George Washington, the crisis of modern life has made us see clearly that we rise or fall together. Because of our English heritage, we Americans have behind us a thousand-year tradition of democratic procedure, of civil liberties, and of those individual rights we take for granted.

Yet, though our political tradition is English, the American people are made up of the most diverse racial elements. If we are not able to work out a foreign policy based on an understanding of other peoples, there is very little reason for us to hope that any other country will be able to do so. In *The American Character* an Englishman explains why this is not as easy as it would seem. Our pioneer heritage, the tensions caused by our minority groups, the desire of second-generation Americans to throw off all European ties, the isolation we once thought we had, all make it hard for us to see that we live in an interdependent world.

The following books indicate that as individuals we are perfectly capable of understanding other people. Turning from an Englishman writing about Americans to an American writing about Englishmen, we have J. Frank Dobie's account of a maverick American professor at large in an English university. Mr. Dobie, who finds now and then that American civilization drives him to the wilds, discovered to his surprise that he was in harmony with English civilization. His delightful book illustrates why.

In the second topic of this meeting we have three American viewpoints on the French. Mary Mian's charming book is a personal record of a highly successful Franco-American alliance. Through her eyes we see her French in-laws, and her life in the French country-side. What we observe with her are people who, aside from superficial differences, are like ourselves. *France,* by Florence Gilliam, deals with various aspects of French art, tradition, and thought, in an attempt to understand the special meaning of France to Americans, and to evaluate the place France may take in the future of Europe.

The books on Latin America introduce us to good neighbors whom we would enjoy knowing better than we do. Formerly the people of the other Americas were far closer to Europe in their interests than they were to us. Today this is no longer true, though it is still true that the average educated Latin American knows far more about our country than we do about his. Although the problems and the needs of the two Americas differ in many respects, this very difference makes possible a stimulating program of cooperation. The exchange of students, U. S. aid in public health programs for the other American countries, and their cooperation in the war effort have brought us closer together.

The flaw in this closeness, as every one knows, is the fascist trend in Argentina. To ignore this serious threat to inter-American solidarity would be most unwise: we must try to understand it and to see that it does not destroy peace in the Americas. There are in the Argentine many people distressed over the fascist bias in their country; how helpless they are, however, has been shown in the recent elections.

1. The English and Us

The American Character, by D. W. Brogan
A Texan in England, by J. Frank Dobie

Sum up briefly Dr. Brogan's interpretation of American attitudes towards world political and economic problems; our pioneer heritage, the effect of our broad and varied continent, problems of minority groups, and the force of educational and religious traditions.

Compare Dr. Brogan's book with Frank Dobie's delightful account of his year in England. How does each writer illustrate certain differences between Englishmen and Americans?

Sum up Mr. Dobie's analysis of the difference between university education in England and in the United States, between English and American students. What are the causes and the results of this difference? Discuss the intellectual freedom of the English universities, the anti-liberal atmosphere of certain American regents, the "German Ph.D. strait jacket," our "unannounced but pervasive fascism," the "incivilities of civil servants."

2. AMERICANS LOOKING AT FRANCE

Immortal Village, by Donald Culross Peattie

Sketch briefly the 2000-year history of the little French village of Vence.

Tell something about the blends of peoples that make up the French race.

My Country-in-Law, by Mary Mian

Read selections of Mary Mian's beautifully understanding book about her family life on a French farm, especially those dealing with this American girl's attempt to bring up her baby "by the book" under circumstances entirely unforeseen by Children's Bureau authors.

France, by Florence Gilliam

What does Miss Gilliam believe is the special importance of the French for Americans and their special contribution to a European civilization? Discuss the chief contemporary arts in France: ballet, theater, painting, poetry.

How may American expatriates and French exiles affect the culture of their own countries? What does Miss Gilliam believe will be the future of France in the development of a world government?

3. BETWEEN US AMERICANS

Latin America in the Future World, by Soule, Efron, and Ness

Guide to the Peace, by Sumner Welles

Using a large wall-map to introduce our chief Latin Neighbors, give briefly their background of colonial economic policy, and their basic problems: purchasing power, literacy, public health and housing, ownership of land and industries, one-crop agriculture, social and political status of labor. What effect had the war on these basic problems?

Discuss our earlier foreign policy towards the countries of Latin America, the formulation of the Good Neighbor policy and its successes.

Discuss: why the United States would serve its own advantage by assisting in the development of a more varied and productive economy in Latin America and how this can best be done; three unsuitable postwar policies, and a recommended development policy, guided by national and international planning agencies; forecast of economic relations between the Americas and of coming land reforms in Latin America.

Additional Reading:

Music of Latin America, by Nicolas Slonimsky, is a very full and competent discussion of music and modern musicians in the twenty Latin American republics. Where Latin-American recordings are available, it could be used as the basis of a musical program.

CHAPTER V

WHAT DO WE WANT FOR AMERICA?

"Where there is no vision the people perish."

In a book reviewed in a later chapter Marshall Field says that our present social and economic system will serve us only if we adapt it to four current needs: "groceries" (by which he means reasonable economic security), peace, access to facts, and toughness in attacking powerful undemocratic elements in America. Peace, the indispensable element, has been the topic of preceding chapters; the necessity for tolerance and civil liberty will appear in later ones. Groceries for everyone, to reduce the matter to its simplest terms, is the problem considered by the authors of the books used here.

To plan or not to plan for reasonable economic security for everyone is hardly a question at the present, though some belated thinkers still argue the point in press and radio. A candid examination of pending legislation should reveal even to the purblind the fact that national planning is here, whether we fear it or not, and is probably here as permanently as the once violently resisted horseless carriage. The remaining questions are: what choice of plans do we have? What are our most urgent needs? What can we afford?

First let us see what we already have. John Wharton's book, *The Theory and Practice of Earning a Living,* is a simple exposition of American capitalism, explaining the difference between capitalism, socialism, and communism. "Free enterprise gave millions of people a chance to get a fair return for the goods and services they produced during that period when the number of potential customers increased with each generation," says Mr. Wharton. He then explains why this system cannot be depended upon today, concluding optimistically, "American ingenuity has usually been able to solve any problems if enough people want a solution to be found and have *sufficient education* to understand the facts which go to make up the problem."

Carl Becker, the late professor emeritus of history at Cornell University, discussed in *Freedom and Responsibility in the American Way of Life* the question as to whether our constitution guaranteed free enterprise to private business. He found upon examining it that it did nothing of the sort. Free enterprise happened to be the way business was normally done in the 18th Century but is no more sacred nor American than any other 18th Century concept. Americans have always been willing for government to regulate business to the extent that public needs make necessary. To the current question: "What choices do we have?" Dr. Becker gave the answer that there are four forms of collectivism ahead of us. Three of these he considered unacceptable to Americans: fascism, communism, and socialism. Americans, he thought, will choose the fourth form: a social democracy which proceeds by democratic methods to take resolute and well considered common action for the common good.

That the English have already taken this step is clear from the examples given by Barbara Wootton, English economist, in *Freedom Under Planning*.

The second question of national planning, "What are our needs?" is considered by Stuart Chase in *Goals for America*. Showing how the "do nothing, plan nothing" school of thought helped bring on the depression after World War I, Mr. Chase names as the chief American domestic problem at present the necessity for a reasonably full employment, which could be assured by attention to American needs in the way of food, shelter, health services, and education.

The third question of planning, "Can we afford what we need?" is analyzed in the books *Aladdin's Lamp* and *Where's the Money Coming From?* and given the answer: "We cannot possibly afford anything less." The thesis of Mr. Munson's book is that the American people could have "an America of material splendor and adventurous living for which only the word Renaissance would be appropriate," if the Aladdin's lamp of credit power were taken out of the hands of private monopoly.

These economists agree that we have in America unrealized levels of resources that could be tapped with no fundamental changes in government or in our system of private ownership. What must be changed, they warn us, is a reactionary resistance to anything new, a tendency to let someone else do the planning for us and a dangerous blindness to the fact that national policies are too often dictated by a few special interests.

1. WHAT CHOICES DO WE HAVE?

Freedom and Responsibility in the American Way of Life, by Carl Becker

Discuss the effect of changing conditions on our freedoms: the relationship between government and business; the four choices available to us; the case for social democracy.

The Theory and Practice of Earning a Living, by John Wharton

Explain the current concept that: ". . . all usable wealth is produced by human effort . . . all tangible wealth comes from the land."

How do cartels and monopolies restrict young people and new industries?

What are the effects of nationalism and industrialism in an interdependent world?

Freedom Under Planning, by Barbara Wootton

Discuss: planning—"the conscious and deliberate choice of economic priorities by some public authority"; the freedom of the consumer to spend and to save; how the unemployed "create unemployment by their lack of the wherewithal either to spend or to save"; possible solutions.

What is political freedom? How can it be reconciled with economic planning? Discuss the use of boards or commissions.

Discuss: "who is to plan the planners," giving Miss Wootton's proposal of small local boards to control officials.

Do you agree that: "it is the citizens of a wisely planned society who are least likely themselves to fall victims to the dangers of planning."

2. WHAT ARE OUR NEEDS?

Goals for America, by Stuart Chase

Summarize chapters 1 and 2. Discuss our needs: food, shelter, clothing, health service, and education.

Summarize the discussion in chapter 10. Why does Mr. Chase say of TVA: "Every major watershed in the country would benefit by similar treatment?"

Do you agree that our private business machine, employing the profit motive as widely as possible, could come near to filling the full employment bill, with government aid for those necessary jobs that do not offer financial profit: housing, health, sanitation, urban redevelopment, dams and conservation?

3. WHAT CAN WE AFFORD?

Aladdin's Lamp, by Gorham Munson

Explain the author's view that the "Aladdin's lamp" of credit power must be taken out of the hands of private monopoly.

Discuss: steps for preventing the third world war; the proper use of the credit power of the republic.

Where's the Money Coming From? by Stuart Chase

Summarize: how Russia and Germany created public credit; how public credit works; savings in the stock market versus constructive projects like the TVA.

Discuss the principles of war finance, and the treasury idea of a "spending tax" instead of the general sales tax which tends to "soak the poor."

Explain: "I have learned not to identify the national debt with my personal debts"; the three kinds of debt; "four roads to full employment"; the principles of a compensatory economy.

CHAPTER VI

HOW CAN WE GET WHAT WE WANT?

"Once more I proclaim the whole of America for each individual, without exception."—Whitman

"The democracies have got to find a permanent way to full employment, and a way to give their citizens a sense of function, of belonging to the community."—Stuart Chase, *Goals For America*

American women are very deeply concerned by the matter of full employment and full production, upon which adequate family living standards for all depend. Yet a sinister idea is sometimes suggested to us: that for a nation to plan for full employment is to risk a loss of freedom. "Freedom to what?" the hungry may ask.

In *Sixty Million Jobs* Secretary of Commerce Wallace denies that Americans have to choose between bread and freedom, saying that by a type of planning typically American, we could have both. The solution is to produce the goods and services so badly needed by our people. Whatever the cost, this plan would be cheaper than another depression like the last one, with its loss of some 350 billion dollars and an estimated 88 million man-years of production. The cost, if we can judge other possible projects by the yardstick of TVA, need not alarm us unduly.

Mr. Wallace says that our country desperately needs a planned program of land-conservation. *TVA, Democracy on the March* is a case-history showing how such jobs can be done by democratic, decentralized planning, carried on by thousands of citizens' committees. TVA has not only created new electrical power, it has vitalized countless businesses, set innumerable factories to work producing necessary machinery, and transformed a bleak section of America into a green and prosperous area. In a hundred other valleys our rivers are now running loose like the juveniles in our city streets, creating destruction. These rivers could be used like the Tennessee to create cheap power to keep small industries busy. Yet the Missouri Valley Authority bill was killed. Why?

Mr. Chase, in *Men at Work*, puts the matter bluntly: "plan, or retreat to a handicraft culture like that of pre-war India or

China." In his book lies the answer to another of today's urgent
questions: "can the human cogs in America's vast assembly lines
be given some satisfaction in their work?" Mr. Chase cites ex-
periments made in industry which show that neither higher
wages nor shorter hours were as effective in increasing the output of workers as giving them a share in the planning of the
work, and a feeling that they participated in the returns.

Tomorrow's Trade examines the case for free trade and for
uncontrolled export of American goods and concludes that a
sounder policy for 20th Century America would be full production for use, with exports exchanged for goods we need.

1. Full Employment—Versus the Breadline

Sixty Million Jobs, by Henry A. Wallace

Discuss the relation of full employment to our fundamental needs.

How can we "attain this goal without a Planned Economy, without
disastrous inflation, and without an unbalanced budget that will endanger
our national abundance?"

Discuss: the United States as "one of the most backward nations in
education in the world."

Read Secretary Wallace's ten points of essential action. Summarize
"the people's peace."

The sixty million jobs: where are they coming from? Who is going
to pay the wages? Wallace's budget for abundance. What pressure
groups oppose full employment?

Interpret: "we have the manpower and the resources to enable everyone of us to live a fuller life. Why don't we do it?"

Compare Henry Wallace's views with those of Stuart Chase and
John Wharton.

2. Cooperation Versus Cages

Men at Work, by Stuart Chase

Review the Hawthorne studies, explaining the devices used to give
the individual worker a feeling of participation in his job. Explain how
these workers "stayed in the factory but came out of the cage."

The work of the Labor-Management Committees; today's critical
shortage in the intelligent management of men; "the folklore of the workers." Tell the story of the one hundred sharecroppers.

3. APPLYING OUR AMERICAN "KNOW HOW"

TVA—Democracy on the March, by David E. Lilienthal

Explain the fundamental purpose of the Tennessee Valley Authority, the method of planning, how politics was kept out, what TVA accomplished.

Discuss decentralized planning; TVA's responsibility for results as well as for the plan; positive versus negative legislation.

Explain TVA's larger implications; TVA and world reconstruction.

4. PRODUCTION FOR USE RATHER THAN EXPORT

Tomorrow's Trade, by Stuart Chase

Explain: "Science is fostering self-sufficiency," "technology shaping the world into regions of balanced economy." What does Mr. Chase mean by "Boatism," or uncontrollable exports, or "the lost $24 billion"?

Discuss: the USA, powerhouse of production and mechanical know-how; fallacy of a favorable balance of trade; the question: "What can we ship in exchange for what we need?"; the necessity for full employment.

Free trade in the 19th Century; its demands. Contrast 19th and 20th Century Europe.

U. S. and Europe: lend-lease and reconstruction of wrecked Europe; the World State—four alternatives.

Read: American paradoxies.

Give the author's summary and conclusions.

CHAPTER VII

OUR VETERANS AND THE FREEDOMS THEY PAID FOR

"I say that there is an absolute good and absolute bad; for all that unites humanity is good and beautiful; and all that separates humanity is absolutely bad and ugly."—Tolstoy

It may shock some of us to see how the homefront looks to Charles Bolte, an intelligent young veteran viewing it with the fresh vision of a returned traveller. At home this soldier found that the principles for which he had lost a limb were by no means secure even here. At first he did not see what one person could do about it. Someone told him of the Veterans Committee, then in need of a chairman, and man and job found each other. If the views in *The New Veteran* are truly representative, America's political future will be interesting.

Mr. Bolte lays much emphasis upon the importance of the work necessary to mobilize the resources of our communities for a coherent veteran's program, but his real concern is with the lack of real democracy in America, and the racial discrimination found in many communities. The people of Springfield, Massachusetts, resolved some time ago to remedy this un-American bias. *The Springfield Plan* shows how this community bridged the chasm between the idea and the reality of America.

Marshall Field sums up in *Freedom is More Than a Word* his creed that if our democracy is to grow we must have freedom of access to facts, and that if our present social system is to serve, we must adapt it to our current needs.

Though Mr. Field stresses the necessity of subdividing social power so no one group can have over-all control, he feels that the pressure groups described by Stuart Chase in *Democracy Under Pressure* are not too dangerous as long as pressures can be kept relatively even.

1. "Soldiers From the Wars Returning"

The New Veteran, by Charles Bolte

To what extent do you think that Charles Bolte speaks for his generation in the following: the need for an international organization to keep the peace; lack of a clear-cut idea of world cooperation; importance of harmony between the veterans and the other citizens; responsibility of the individual for good government.

Summarize: The Baruch report on Veteran's Administration; the organization plans in Appendix B; the successful veteran's service in Bridgeport, Connecticut.

Additional Reading:

Up Front, by Bill Mauldin
Island 49, by Merle Miller
Keep Your Head Down, by Walter Bernstein
It's Good to be Alive, by Henrietta Bruce Sharon
G. I. Nightingale, by Theresa Archard

2. "DEMOCRACY IS PEOPLE—LIVING TOGETHER AS EQUALS"

The Springfield Plan, by James Waterman Wise

What is the Springfield plan; who originated it? Evaluate results after five years of education in democratic living together. Select representative photographs and give a short synopsis of the text. What parts of the Springfield plan might be adapted for your community? What forces might oppose it?

One Nation, by Wallace Stegner

Using the photos to illustrate the discussion, give the chief problems of the American racial and religious minorities. Read the figures on page 3. Discuss the patterns of exclusion. How does society pay the bill for illnesses and crimes that cannot be segregated in slums?

What is the attitude of the average community, church, and school authorities to these minorities? What steps has your community taken to combat intolerance? How can the individual guard against tabloid thinking?

Discuss: the close relationship between racial and religious intolerance and fascism; how and why the American ideal of "equal rights of opportunity for all" became mislaid. If we fail to solve the problems of minorities in the United States, how can we expect peace in the world of nations?

Additional Reading:

Color and Democracy, by W. E. B. DuBois

3. MEET THE "ME FIRST" BRIGADE!

Democracy Under Pressure, by Stuart Chase

Discuss the special pressure groups in Washington and their monopolistic methods, the special interest formula for a high unit price rather than high production, and the effect of this on employment.

Industrial groups: the housing bloc and its effect on housing; drug and cosmetics laws that fail to protect the consumer; the locking up of inventions; monopolies and their real menace, the restriction of output. Read aloud the author's five conclusions about industrial pressure groups.

Labor: its failure to understand that wartime strikes were a strike against the nation and that the future of labor unions lies in serving community interests as well as shop interests; read "What workers want."

Discuss "big agriculture" and its method of manipulating Congress; back to the land; "big government: who looks after the interests of the people at large?

Freedom Is More Than a Word, by Marshall Field

Discuss the activities of special pressure groups in newspapers and radio; Mr. Field's fight for a free press. Summarize his social philosophy in regard to the individual and the state; four essentials to democracy; dispossessed minorities; technique of peaceful change; to use our credit and tools and American know-how in international cooperation for peace and plenty.

Additional Reading:

Safeguarding Civil Liberty Today, by Becker, Lerner, Fly, Dushman, Biddle, Day

Goodbye to G. I. by Maxwell Droke

Up Front, by Bill Mauldin

CHAPTER VIII

OUR CHILDREN AND THEIR FUTURE

"To be a functioning democracy we must search out the truth
and on this foundation build a decent and humane society."
—David Lilienthal

Agnes Meyer, in *Journey Through Chaos*, gave convincing
evidence that during the war it was "the adolescent child of fif-
teen and under who is being overlooked and economically exploited from one end of our country to the other." Now we must
imagine these young war-workers sent back into a home environ-
ment they have outgrown, outside the school system, no longer
employed, but still retaining tastes given them by their brief
period of money-making. Let's add thousands of demobilized
soldiers whose education was interrupted, and the group of teen-
age youngsters still in school at war's end, and ask ourselves:
"What have our communities to offer these young people to help
them to self-dependent maturity?"

Education for All American Youth gives two previews of what
may happen to them. The first is a fear that our overworked
and understaffed schools will prove so inadequate that the federal
government will take over the control of education, the very field
where centralized authority is most dangerous to democracy.

The second preview is a hope that we may preserve our
locally administered schools by means of federal financial aid,
and that we will remodel them into a continuous program of
vocational, recreational, and civic guidance for everyone who
needs it. This book and the publications of the Children's Bureau
show how women can help reshape their children's future by
studying the local schools and by creating a program of group
care for young children, health services for mothers and children, playgrounds and recreation centers for adults as well as
children: in short, by a closer integration of public and private
welfare work with the school system.

The Children's Bureau has made proposals for a federal and
state cooperation program of child health and care. These proposals, outlined in the publications used in this meeting, are a

working basis for a community plan to serve the needs of children of all ages.

What would this program cost the nation? Probably little more than we are already spending. A recent national conference on child welfare found that at present the federal government is already allotting a few hundred million dollars for programs and services for the children and youth, but that this outlay is scattered through at least 33 uncoordinated and often competing departments.

As for the costs to the individual community, this is a question that can only be answered by other questions: what is the present cost of preventable disease, delinquency, and crime? What is the future value to the community of well-balanced citizens? Which would we rather pay for: useful citizens or destructive ones?

1. TODAY'S TRAINING FOR TOMORROW'S LEADERS

Education for All American Youth, by the Educational Policies Commission

Give briefly the "History That Should Not Happen." Discuss the "Five Years After the War" blue-prints for tomorrow which most fit your community. For example: The Farmville Community School—its continuous program; educational plans for students; guidance; productive work experiences; education for civic competence, for personal development of youth; the school's continuing responsibility. Read the seven principles set up for program planning.

If your community is in a city, discuss the Schools for Youth in American City.

Reasons for strengthening our state and local school systems with decentralized Federal assistance. System of youth education in the ideal state, "Columbia."

Summarize: The History that Must be Written.

Twenty Careers of Tomorrow, by Darrell and Frances Huff

How may people prepare for a career in these fields: Chemistry—synthetic materials, glass, plastics, and foods; electronics; transportation—flying flivvers; communications—television and publishing; housing.

Discuss: "College or hard knocks?", "You may not need the college, but you need the education." How can the young person discover coming occupations and avoid dying industries and trades?

Science Today and Tomorrow, by Waldemar Kaempffert

Summarize, "Blueprint of a future suburb"; impact of science technology on human life; science discovers brain waves; "sick medicine needs a doctor." What does science tell about the future of man and the universe?

Additional Reading:

Science Yearbook of 1945, edited by John D. Ratcliff (see new developments in treatment of mental disease)

2. CO-ORDINATION BEGINS WITH THE HOME COMMUNITY

State and Community Planning for Children and Youth, Children's Bureau
Building the Future for Children and Youth, Children's Bureau
Some Principles for Consideration in State and Community Planning for the Needs of Children, Children's Bureau

Community Planning on Group Care of Children, Bulletin No. 2

Give the evidence of the need for Federal assistance in a service for maternal and child health. Summarize the proposals of the Children's Bureau for such a program.

Write your Representatives for recent news on pending legislation. What has happened to the Doyle Bill? HR 4202? S1050? S1318? (for welfare services needed.)

What child-health and child-care services are needed in your community? Is there a planning group for such services? What could your club do to further this work? Study carefully the recommendations given for the formation of such a community council.

CHAPTER IX

THE HOMEMAKER LOOKS AT HEALTH AND HOUSING

"The state is going to insist, fifty years from now, on good health, insist on it as a right of what is known as the sovereignty of the people."—Franklin Roosevelt

Although the words of our late president "I see one-third of the nation ill-housed, ill-clad, ill-nourished" are perhaps an understatement of our national needs at present, in one field at least change is coming with a rapidity that may endanger the successful working of the legislative plan. President Truman insists even now that every American citizen has the right to adequate medical care and to protection from the economic losses of sickness. He advocates a national health program that will include expanded public health, maternal and child health services, the construction of hospitals, and government support of medical costs through an extension of present insurance systems. The legislation covering these general principles should be carefully charted.

National medical associations fighting the idea of public medicine may face the reality itself, emerging from Congress before adequate plans have been worked out in the states and communities. Meanwhile, however, there are valuable projects which can be carried out in local communities such as those described in the North Carolina Health Bulletins.

Housing is a complex subject not adequately covered by any one book now available. Its importance to health and happiness cannot be over-emphasized. A housing program to fit our needs would aid tremendously in the reconversion of our industries. *A Million Homes a Year,* by Dorothy Rosenman, tells how science and business could help rehabilitate slum areas and recommends a program of government housing for low-income families.

That we will never have decent housing until the whole structure of our society is remodeled is the thesis of *When Democracy Builds.* A house is a man's best tool for a satisfactory life, says Frank Lloyd Wright, and as yet we have never used our inventive genius to give a satisfactory life to all the people. Mr. Wright loathes the "deadly boxing" of present slum-clearance projects. Such works result only "in putting off by mitigation of a horror the day of regeneration for the actual poor." Though we may prefer dull monotonous "boxing" to disease-breeding slums, there is a sober truth in the view that such measures make a respectable institution of the poverty we should consider a national disgrace.

For his city of the future, Mr. Wright would create a decentralized community of small homes and food-providing gardens, within reach of factories and other places of work. This cure for the modern disease of ant-hill life might be possible even now, if our machinery were put to work for the people. We don't have that $1500 prefabricated house we have been promised so long, he says, because inventions are suppressed and the benefit of the 'cheapening' process is not passed on to the consumer.

1. COMING EVENTS IN HEALTH CARE

Health Instruction Yearbook, 1944, compiled by Oliver E. Byrd

> Discuss "Health as a Social Problem"; warborn diseases, current legislation and conferences on nutrition, fatigue, venereal diseases, pure food and drugs, family health, and community health services.
>
> Probabilities in a Federal program of medical care and public health services. Senator Wagner's analysis of the Wagner-Murray-Dingell bill. To what extent is organized public health responsible for improved health? Summarize the need for a greatly expanded public health service.

Public Medical Care, by Franz Goldman

> Discuss "adequate medical care is a fundamental human right: "It is as much a necessity of life as food, shelter, clothing or education." Sum up the history of public medical facilities and services. Who are the "medically indigent"? Health insurance versus all-out state medicine. Administrative problems of public health care, especially in rural areas. Display the North Carolina Public Health pamphlets and discuss the public health facilities of your community and their need. What about community plans for efficient use of future public funds?

2. HOUSING: TODAY'S REALITY AND TOMORROW'S POSSIBILITIES

"We shape our buildings, then our buildings shape our lives."

—Winston Churchill

A Million Homes a Year, by Dorothy Rosenman

> Discuss the conclusions of this author in Chapter XI. Three goals of modern planning for housing: 1) homes at lower cost, 2) stabilizing

values by zoning regulations and neighborhood development, 3) convenient, prosperous and pleasurable settings.

Discuss: slums and blighted areas; legislation toward town planning; the regional planning organizations; "own your own?"

Federal housing, trial and errors. What are the alternatives?

When Democracy Builds, by Frank Lloyd Wright

Give the author's views on the following: the faults of our housing are due to the faults of our society itself: 1) centralization, and the life of the ant-heap, and 2) the major economic artificialities, rent for money, rent for land, traffic in invention, and survivals of feudal despotism in American society.

The cure: 1) a realization of the deadly nature of machine power, either in mechanics or in the organization of industry and government; 2) effort from within the individual.

Explain: "rugged individualism" differs from democratic individuality as license differs from liberty; the city and the forces beginning to destroy it—the awakening of the wandering instinct in man, with modern increased mobility and the annihilation of distance; how these forces will affect the city of the future.

Describe and show the models of the Usonian farm, the Usonian factory district. Discuss pioneer decentralization, the mobile hotel and motor-houses; the community center, hospitals and universities and public schools—more and more capable teachers and always smaller and smaller flocks.

Mr. Wright's idea that cities destroyed by bombs may be rebuilt in such a way that they will be better than our own; his message to young architects.

Additional Reading:

Building or Buying a House, by B. K. Johnstone. (The complete home-
   builder's guide, from site selection to house construction.)

Tomorrow's House, by George Nelson and Henry Wright

CHAPTER X

ARE WOMEN PEOPLE?

"He who tries to do people good stands knocking at the door,
but he who loves finds the door open."—Tagore

The question of woman and her place, though less productive of bloodshed than others considered in this course, has caused enormous quantities of ink to flow. Mary R. Beard gives the background of this question in *Woman as Force in History* and Dr. Ernest R. Groves in *The American Woman*. Nineteenth century orators of platform and fireside traditionally made the welkin ring with pronouncements that woman's place was in the home and that once outside this refuge, she was outclassed by man in practically all respects. Mrs. Beard makes a study of the traditions concerning the relationship between men and women, and tests them by economic, intellectual, and social history. Her conclusions are interesting and somewhat surprising.

Several generations of defiant women hurled themselves against the limitations imposed by the Victorian concept and succeeded in broadening woman's opportunities, aided by that change in human efficiency called the Industrial Revolution.

Mrs. Beard questions, however, the viewpoint of those feminists who believe that all inequalities would be ironed out if the sexes were given equal education and opportunities. Though this theory has never been fully tested, it may conflict somewhat with the biological realities made clear in Amram Scheinfeld's *Women and Men*. Food and clothing no longer make a virtual slavery in the individual home necessary, but modern career women have found that children remain handicraft products, and that working mothers have a difficult double role.

During the war, however, it became necessary for millions of women to go to work in a vast assembly line. Their children were put in nursery schools, or left in the care of neighbors. As Susan B. Anthony II shows in *Out of the Kitchen—Into the War*, women proved beyond doubt that they could do "man's work" and do it well, though no real effort was made to give competent American professional women the responsibilities they could have met. Miss Anthony shows how these women workers carried a double load, handicapped by archaic methods of house-keeping and child-care, by inequality of opportunity and pay, and by the opposition of reactionary political and social leaders.

Yet somewhere in this vast war experience, in England or Russia if not here, must lie a few of the answers to old questions about the most effective use of woman-power in civilization. When women left their individual homes, did they and their families lose or gain by it? Were their children better off in good nursery schools than in haphazard, non-child-centered homes? How can homemakers best use the free time resulting from new electrical equipment and processed foods? Finally, what are the real differences in the capacities of men and women, and how can they work together to prevent the giant catastrophe that faces modern nations, glaring at each other over their atomic bomb stock-piles?

One answer to the last question lies in the constructive use we could make of our social and professional clubs and nation-wide citizens' organizations. The books and bulletins discussed below give a complete technique for the efficient use by community organizations of such tools as publications, radio, lectures and the press.

1. WOMAN, WHEREFORE ART THOU WOMAN?

Woman as Force In History, by Mary R. Beard

> Trace briefly the chief traditions in regard to women: that she has been a "subject sex" throughout history, that the world has always been "a man's world," and that "equality" is the goal of women.
>
> What are Mrs. Beard's conclusions as to the validity of these concepts?
>
> Discuss: "Women have done far more than exist and bear and rear children. They have played a great role in directing human events as thought and action. Women have been a force in making all the history that has been made."

Women and Men, by Amram Scheinfeld

"The Legal Status of Women," Bulletin No. 157, Women's Bureau

> Sum up the basic differences between women and men; according to statistics, which is "the weaker sex"? Discuss the differences in intelligence, and in chronological and biological ages: in what fields do boys and girls excel respectively?

How do the problems of adolescence differ in girls and boys? Has our educational system taken these differences into account?

What has the Soviet found in its attempt to abolish inequality between men and women? Discuss: "What seems to be in order is an overhauling in our whole concept and institutions of male dominance. The question is how far it should be or could be carried."

2. WASTED WOMAN-POWER

Out of the Kitchen—Into the War, by Susan B. Anthony

Why does the author say that women are their own jailers? What does she mean by "Jim-Crowisms for Women"?

Give the story of the feminist struggle. Contrast the theories of John Stuart Mill and Lewis Henry Morgan about the role of women.

Discuss briefly the chief problems faced by working women: why there are so few women in policy-making positions and professional jobs; labor's failure to recognize the importance of nursery schools and other aids to working women; why nurseries are a national problem; the professional woman's lack of recognition and equal pay; women's failure to understand their problems; the stand of the National Federation of Business and Professional Women, and the report of the NRPB.

Discuss fully the "Equal Rights Amendment," the central purpose of which is to abolish minimum wage orders and maximum hour laws for women in the 48 states. What bill is needed?

3. ORGANIZING FOR CITIZENSHIP

Take Your Place at the Peace Table, by Edward L. Bernays

Methods of community organization. What use can be made of such aids as publications, radio, motion pictures, the press? What are the chief objectives of the women's organizations in your community?

Women's Opportunities and Responsibilities in Citizenship, by George B. Cutten

Summarize the material in this very concrete and specific discussion of women as citizens.

Here's How It's Done, by Florence B. Widutis

Discuss: formation of community study groups; the community council; use of speakers, records, films, and other visual aids.

How to use the full resources of your community; of local, state and federal agencies. (Note the directory of organizations furnishing materials and speakers.)

Your public: letters to the press, advertising, radio.

CHAPTER XI

PSYCHOLOGY FOR HOMEMAKERS

"Unawareness of the psychological forces that govern our conduct is probably the greatest barrier to the healthy, happy adjustment of individuals to society. We must understand these if we are to learn how to work and live together beautifully."
—From *Bringing Up Ourselves*, by Helen Gibson Hogue

It is a curious fact that while our generation takes it for granted that man can weigh the stars and release the mysterious force in the atom, we continue to shake our heads and say, "you can't change human nature!" In other fields we believe in investigation and measurement. School children study what happens when you mix two chemicals together, but adults fail to realize that if two people (or two countries) form explosive mixtures under certain circumstances, bad emotional training rather than immutable laws are at fault.

At a time when divorce has become almost impossible in the Soviet Union, in our own country it has increased from the 1 to 9 ratio of prewar years towards a predicted high of one divorce for every four marriages. Divorce and broken homes with their heart-breaking train of warped childhood and juvenile delinquency are symptomatic of some deep disturbance in our way of living which we should do well to try to understand.

During his three decades of marriage counselling and teaching, Dr. Ernest Groves has written various helpful books on preparation for and adjustment within marriage. In the handbook listed below he deals competently with specific problems that lead to divorce and others that arise during and after divorce.

One disturbing feature of modern life is the breaking down of society into the unit of the small family. Homemakers and communities must find wholesome ways to satisfy the individual's need to feel that he is a member of a group, a need so cleverly exploited by the fascist masters. Dr. Reilly and Margery Wilson offer practical suggestions for creating harmonious team-work in the family and in the community.

Psychiatrists know that most of the problems of marriage arise from psychic rather than physical causes, that marriage

failures are often a result of personalities warped by earlier experiences. *Bringing Up Ourselves,* by Helen Gibson Hogue,
shows with extraordinary skill and insight how these personality
distortions are almost inevitably passed on from one generation
to another unless parents make an effort to understand them.
Every community needs a psychiatric clinic as desperately as it
needs good doctors and dentists. Until this realization is more
general, however, books may offer the only possible outside aid
for problems immensely more significant than toothaches or other
minor ills.

1. "HOW DO YOU GET THAT WAY!"

Bringing Up Ourselves, by Helen Gibson Hogue

Discuss fully the author's emphasis on the need to understand rather
than to punish aggressive children, the danger of the Jehovah complex
in parents. Give the laws that govern the development of our emotions,
stressing the importance of affection and recognition in the development
of personality. Results of the Yale Institute study of delinquency in
children; the necessity of building satisfactory relations; the three types
of personality. How to resolve tensions creatively, to avoid the "repeat
pattern." Give the author's views on the psychological preparation for
work and for marriage.

2. RELATIONS AND RELATIONSHIPS

How to Improve Your Human Relations, by William J. Reilly

Give Dr. Reilly's "rules for straight thinking" (p. 186). Summarize his application of these rules to the problems of professional contacts and social acquaintances. Discuss "family business meetings."
Explain his use of "sponsors."

Interpret the author's "one sure way to open a mind . . .", "The ful-
filling law of human relations is to give more than you get from anyone."

The Woman You Want to Be, by Margery Wilson

Give the philosophy underlying Miss Wilson's suggestions for the
cultivation of social ease. Explain: "with an almost startling degree of
accuracy, we receive from life what we unconsciously demand." Discuss
the author's view that results in life are obtained through working from
within, not from without, and that you can stay where you are and
change your life and yourself almost beyond recognition.

3. MARRIAGE IS AS MARRIAGE DOES

When You Marry, by Evelyn M. Duval and Reuben Hill

Make your own selection from the contents of this book. Discuss in detail part 4: Family Life Today, Yesterday, and Tomorrow. In what ways is family life changing? How does this effect the status of women? What is the role of women in developing a feeling for world citizenship?

Effect of the war on marriage trends; on juvenile delinquency? How can women best help the returning service men of their family?

Discuss the common conflicts of marriage. Tell something about marital counselling services. From the many other excellent discussions in this book, make whatever other selections you feel would appeal to the members of your club.

4. AID FOR AILING MARRIAGES

Conserving Marriage and the Family, by Ernest R. Groves

Give briefly this marriage counsellor's summary of the most common reasons why marriages fail. Motives that are not usually recognized: father or mother fixation, failure to grow up, monotony.

Discuss: the sources of chronic irritability; "in-law trouble and its real roots; the American woman's career conflict; therapy for ailing marriages.

CHAPTER XII

AND ONE TO GROW ON!

"So far in the history of the world there have never been enough mature people in the right places."—Major General George B. Chisholm, Canadian Psychiatrist

The books reviewed in this course make it entirely clear that the preservation and application of the democratic ideals we value will require the cooperation of every mature mind available. Unhappily, the maturity of the individual's mind may depend somewhat upon the spiritual atmosphere of the society in which it develops, or fails to develop. E. B. White expresses this closed circuit with polished perfection in *One Man's Meat*. He traces much of our restlessness, our pursuit of cheap diversions that cause expensive erosion of mind and spirit, to a fundamental unfairness that has developed in our economic structure, an illness of society itself: the failure to resolve the vital question of the relationship of man to the state, and of men towards each other.

What the common man wanted and never got, says Mr. White (chilling the reader with his use of the past tense) was a share in the excitement, a sense of participation in the returns from our free enterprise: in short, a hand in the game. That even the most fortunate cannot escape the consequences of this unfairness is the astringent medicine underneath Mr. White's delightful foolery about farm animals whose life hangs by a hair and birds which must be identified at inconvenient seasons.

From this season's spate of books advising the individual how to adjust to a society molded largely by an uncreative cynicism calling itself "realism," we choose two with somewhat opposing viewpoints. Mrs. Ray makes a good case for her belief that the solution of an individual's problems lies in an energetic program of work and recreation. The neuro-psychiatrists, however, warn us that nervousness and its usual companion, anhedonia (an uncommon word for the too-common inability to be happy) cause physical illnesses and tensions that must be dissolved through relaxation of tense muscles, as well as through a conscious attack on the sub-conscious emotional problems that cause adults to behave in an immature way. Since it has been estimated that some 80% of the people who go to doctors suffer from troubles that arise from nervous rather than from organic causes, this technique would be worth mastering. Unfortunately, says Dr. Fink, most people are satisfied with half-way measures and will not persist long enough to complete either their understanding or their relaxation.

This is a common human failing not confined to our own troubled times. Looking in his heart four hundred years ago, Sir Frances Drake found the only remedy for it, in words as pertinent now as they were then: "O Lord God, when Thou givest to Thy servants to endeavor any great matter, grant us also to know that it is not the beginning but the continuing of the same, until it is thoroughly finished, which yieldeth the true glory."

1. INTEREST—THE FOUNTAIN OF YOUTH

How Never to be Tired, by Marie Beynon Ray

Discuss: the author's thesis that energy is the secret of success and that everyone possesses unused reserves of energy; the chief causes of fatigue,—boredom, indecision, and unresolved emotional tensions; habit in the conquest of fatigue.

How to vanquish fatigue: "if you feel tired, act energetic and you will soon feel energetic." To outwit boredom: "interest in our work is the greatest single factor in human happiness." "Interesting people are people who are interested. Bores are people who are bored."

Additional Reading:

Creative Hands, by Cox and Weissman, a discussion of handicrafts that may furnish family hobbies and enrich home-life.

Now That We Have to Walk, by Raymond Tifft Fuller, a log of out-of-doors pleasures for the amateur naturalist.

Music for Your Health, by Edward Podolsky, a study of the use of music in physical and mental therapy and in increasing personal effectiveness.

Pastimes for the Patient, by Marguerite Ickis, occupations for the invalid, from nature-study, music, painting, to games and crafts.

2. RECREATION IS NOT RELAXATION

Release From Nervous Tension, by David Harold Fink

Your Nerves, How to Release Emotional Tensions, by Louis E. Bisch

Discuss: the contention of these doctors that nervousness is a physical disease caused largely by emotional tensions, and can be cured by understanding and by relaxation; why people fail to resolve their ten-

sions: failure to understand emotional nature and the causes for re-
pressions, and the failure to get started.

Discuss: what is meant by "compromise adjustment," by the role
of frustration in nervousness, by the influence of the interbrain on
health?

Explain Dr. Fink's technique of self-analysis and of muscle relaxation.

Interpret: "Human beings have no instincts. Their bodily activities are infinitely plastic. Social situations are the forces that give human activities their direction and drive. Diversion is not relaxation.
Recreation is not relaxation. Only relaxation is: "do anything in which
you are, or used to be, interested."

Additional Reading:

How to Get and Keep Good Health, by Stella Regina Dolan

3. LOVE LETTER TO AMERICA—WITH RESERVATIONS

One Man's Meat, by E. B. White

Read aloud some of your favorite passages in this book: e. g., in-
terruption by feathered friends (284); "domestic memorandum" (317).

Give Mr. White's view as to the true nature of "The Wave of the
Future" (205). Read some of his passages on intolerance. Give the
theme of his essay on Control.

Mr. White on the common man; on international alliances; on our
feeling for America.

Tell the story of Aunt Poo: "Hate is a mere beginner of wars. To
end them we shall have to marry our indignation with our faith."

SPECIAL REFERENCE BIBLIOGRAPHY

Anthony, Susan B.	*Out of the Kitchen into the War.* 1944. (10)	Stephen	$2.50
Arne, Sigrid	*United Nations Primer.* 1945. (1)	Rinehart	1.00
Beard, M. R.	*Woman as Force in History.* 1946. (10)	Macmillan	3.50
Becker, Carl	*Freedom and Responsibility.* 1945. (5)	Knopf	2.50
Bernays, E. L.	*Take Your Place at the Peace Table.* 1945. (10)	Duell	1.00
Bisch, L. E.	*Your Nerves.* 1945. (12)	Funk	2.50
Bolte, C. G.	*The New Veteran.* 1945. (7)	Reynal	2.00
Brogan, D. W.	*The American Character.* 1944. (4)	Knopf	2.50
Byrd, O. E.	*Health Instruction Yearbook.* 1944. (9)	Stanford	3.00
Chase, Stuart	*Democracy Under Pressure.* 1945. (7)	Twentieth	1.00
Chase, Stuart	*Goals for America.* 1942. (5)	Twentieth	1.00
Chase, Stuart	*Men at Work.* 1945. (6)	Harcourt	2.00
Chase, Stuart	*Tomorrow's Trade.* 1945. (6)	Twentieth	1.00
Chase, Stuart	*Where's the Money Coming From?* 1943. (5)	Twentieth	1.00
Children's Bureau	*State and Community Planning for Children.*	U. S. Dept. Labor	free
Children's Bureau	*Building the Future for Children.* (8)	U. S. Dept. Labor	free
Children's Bureau	*Some Principles for Consideration in State and Community Planning for Children.* (8)	U. S. Dept. Labor	free
	Community Planning on Group Care of Children. (8)	Nat. Com.	.15
Cort, David	*The Great Union.* 1944. (1)	Union Press	
Cutten, G. B.	*Women's Opportunities & Responsibilities.* 1945. (10)	Woman's F.	free
Dobie, J. F.	*A Texan in England.* 1945. (4)	Little	2.50
Duval & Hill	*When You Marry.* 1945. (11)	Ass'n. Pr.	3.00
	Education for All American Youth. 1945. (8)	Edu. Pol. Com.	1.00
Field, Marshall	*Freedom Is More than a Word.* 1945. (7)	Univ. of Chicago	2.50
Fink, D. H.	*Release from Nervous Tension.* 1944. (12)	Simon	2.00
Forman, Harrison	*Report from Red China.* 1945. (3)	Holt	3.00
Gilliam, Florence	*France.* 1945. (4)	Dutton	2.50
Goldman, Franz	*Public Medical Care.* 1945. (9)	Columbia	2.75
Groves, E. R.	*The American Woman.* 1944. (10)	Emerson	3.50

Groves, E. R.	*Conserving Marriage and the Family.* 1944. (11)	Macmillan	1.75
Guerard, Albert	*Europe: Free and United.* 1945. (2)	Stanford	2.50
Hogue, H. G.	*Bringing Up Ourselves.* 1943. (11)	Scribner's	1.50
Huff, D. & F.	*Twenty Careers of Tomorrow.* 1945. (8)	Whittlesey	2.50
Kaempffert, W. B.	*Science Today & Tomorrow.* 1945. (8)	Viking	2.75
Lanux, Pierre de	*European Manifest.* 1945. (1)	Creative	2.00
Lauterbach, R. E.	*These Are the Russians.* 1945. (3)	Harper	3.00
Lilienthal, D. E.	*TVA—Democracy on the March.* 1945. (6)	Harper	2.50
Ludwig, Emil	*The Moral Conquest of Germany.* 1945. (2)	Doubleday	2.00
Mian, Mary	*My Country-in-Law.* 1946. (4)	Houghton	2.50
Munson, Gorham	*Aladdin's Lamp.* 1945. (5)	Creative	3.75
Peattie, D. C.	*Immortal Village.* 1945. (4)	Univ. of Chicago	3.00
Peffer, Nathaniel	*America's Place in the World.* 1945. (1)	Viking	2.75
Ray, M. B.	*How Never to Be Tired.* 1945. (12)	Bobbs	2.50
Reilly, W. J.	*How to Improve Your Human Relations.* 1944. (11)	Harper	2.50
Reves, Emery	*The Anatomy of Peace.* 1945. (1)	Harper	2.00
Rosenman, Dorothy	*A Million Homes a Year.* 1945. (9)	Harcourt	3.50
Rowe, D. N.	*China Among the Powers.* 1945. (3)	Harcourt	2.00
Sayers & Kahn	*The Plot Against the Peace.* 1945. (2)	Dial	2.75
Scheinfeld, Amram	*Women and Men.* 1944. (10)	Harcourt	3.50
Snow, Edgar	*Pattern of Soviet Power.* 1945. (3)	Random	2.75
Snow, Edgar	*People on Our Side.* 1944. (3)	Random	3.50
Soule, Efron, Ness	*Latin America in Future World.* 1945. (4)	Rinehart	3.50
Stegner, Wallace	*One Nation.* 1945. (7)	Houghton	3.75
Tolischus, O. D.	*Through Japanese Eyes.* 1945. (2)	Reynal	2.00
Tong, H. K.	*China After Seven Years of War.* 1945. (3)	Macmillan	2.00
Wallace, H. A.	*Sixty Million Jobs.* 1945. (6)	Reynal	1.00
Warburg, J. P.	*Foreign Policy Begins at Home.* 1944. (1)	Harcourt	2.50
Welles, Sumner	*Guide to the Peace.* 1945. (4)	Dryden	3.75
Wharton, J. F.	*Theory and Practice of Earning a Living.* 1945. (5)	Simon	2.50
White, E. B.	*One Man's Meat.* 1948. (12)	Harper	2.75
Widutis, F. V.	*Here's How It's Done.* (10)	Postwar Inf.	
Wilson, Margery	*The Woman You Want to Be.* 1943. (11)	Lippincott	2.95
Wise, J. W.	*The Springfield Plan.* 1945. (7)	Viking	2.50
Wootton, Barbara	*Freedom Under Planning.* 1945. (5)	UNC Press	2.00
Wright, F. L.	*When Democracy Builds.* 1945. (9)	Univ. of Chicago	4.00

ADDITIONAL REFERENCES

Archard, Theresa	*G. I. Nightingale.* 1945. (7)	Norton	$2.50
Becker, Carl	*Safeguarding Civil Liberty Today.* 1945. (7)	Cornell	2.00
Bernstein, Walter	*Keep Your Head Down.* 1945. (7)	Viking	2.00
Buchanan, S. L.	*Legal Status of Women in U. S.* (10)	U. S. Dept. Labor	.15
Callendar, Harold	*A Preface to Peace.* 1944. (1)	Knopf	3.00
Cox & Weismann	*Creative Hands.* 1945. (12)	Wiley	3.75
De Roussy de Sales	*Making of Tomorrow.* 1942. (1)	Reynal	3.00
Dolan, S. R.	*How to Get and Keep Good Health.* 1945. (12)	Ackerman	2.00
Droke, Maxwell	*Good-by to G. I.* 1945. (7)	Abingdon	1.00
DuBois, W. E. B.	*Color and Democracy.* 1945. (7)	Harcourt	2.00
Fuller, Raymond	*Now That We Have to Walk.* 1944. (12)	Dutton	2.50
Groves, E. R.	*The American Woman.* 1944. (10)	Emerson	3.50
Ickis, Marguerite	*Pastimes for the Patient.* 1945. (12)	Barnes	3.00
Johnstone, B. K.	*Building or Buying a House.* 1945. (9)	McGraw	2.75
	Legal Status of Women in U. S. (10)	Women's Bureau	.15
Mauldin, Bill	*Up Front.* 1945. (7)	Holt	3.00
Miller, Merle	*Island 49.* 1945. (7)	Crowell	2.00
Nelson & Wright	*Tomorrow's House.* 1945. (9)	Simon	2.50
Podolsky, Edward	*Music for Your Health.* 1945. (12)	Ackerman	3.75
Ratcliff, J. D.	*Science Year Book of 1945.* 1945. (8)	Doubleday	2.50
Sharon, H. B.	*It's Good to Be Alive.* 1945. (7)	Dodd	2.00
Slonimsky, Nicolas	*Music of Latin America.* 1945. (4)	Harcourt	2.50
Warburg, J. P.	*Foreign Policy Begins at Home.* 1944. (2)	Crowell	3.50
Welles, Sumner	*A Time for Decision.* 1944. (1)	Harper	3.00
Whiteleather, M.	*Main Streets New Neighbors.* 1945. (2)	Lippincott	3.00
Visson, André	*Coming Struggle for Peace.* 1944. (2)	Viking	3.00

ADDRESSES OF PUBLISHERS

Abingdon-Cokesbury, 819 Broadway, Nashville 2.
Ackerman (Bernard) Inc., 381 Fourth Ave., New York 16.
Association Press, 347 Madison Ave., New York 17.
Barnes (A. S.) & Co., 67 W. 44th St., New York 18.
Columbia University Press, 2960 Broadway, New York 27.
Crowell (Thomas &.) Co., 432 Fourth Ave., New York 16.
Dryden Press, 386 Fourth Ave., New York 16.
Harcourt, Brace & Co., Inc., 383 Madison Ave., New York 17.
Harper & Bros., 49 E. 33rd St., New York 16.
Holt (Henry) & Co., Inc., 257 Fourth Ave., New York 10.
Houghton Mifflin Co., 2 Park St., Boston 7.
Knopf (Alfred A.), Inc., 501 Madison Ave., New York 22.
Lippincott (J. B.) Co., 227 S. 6th St., Philadelphia 5.
Little, Brown & Co., 34 Beacon St., Boston 6.
McGraw-Hill Book Co., Inc., 330 W. 42nd St., New York 18.
Macmillan Co., 60 Fifth Ave., New York 11.
National Committee on Group Care of Children, Room 911, 119 W. 578,
    New York 19.
Norton (W. W.) & Co., Inc., 70 Fifth Ave., New York 11.
Random House, Inc., 20 E. 57th St., New York 22.
Reynal & Hitchcock, Inc., 8 W. 40th St., New York 18.
Rinehart, Inc., 232 Madison Ave., New York 16.
Scribner's (Charles) Sons, 597 Fifth Ave., New York 17.
Simon & Schuster, Inc., 1230 Sixth Ave., New York 20.
Stanford University Press, Stanford University, Cal.
Stephen Daye, Inc., 48 E. 43rd St., New York 17.
Twentieth Century Fund, Inc., 330 W. 42nd St., New York 18.
Union Press, 700 9th St., Washington 1, D. C.
University of Chicago Press, 5750 Ellis Ave., Chicago 37.
University of North Carolina Press, Chapel Hill.
Viking Press, Inc., 18 E. 48th St., New York 17.
Whittlesey House. See McGraw-Hill.
Wiley (John) & Sons, Inc., 440 Fourth Ave., New York 16.
Woman's Foundation, 10 E. Fortieth St., New York.
Women's Bureau, U. S. Department of Labor, Washington, D. C.

SCHEDULE OF MEETINGS

Eleventh Meeting: PSYCHOLOGY FOR HOMEMAKERS
1. "How Do You Get That Way!"
2. Relations and Relationships
3. Marriage Is As Marriage Does
4. Aid for Ailing Marriages

Twelfth Meeting: AND ONE TO GROW ON!
1. Interest—The Fountain of Youth
2. Recreation is Not Relaxation
3. Love Letter to America—with Reservations

THE UNIVERSITY OF NORTH CAROLINA
LIBRARY EXTENSION DEPARTMENT

The Library Extension Department of the University Library is maintained for the purpose of bringing to the citizens of North Caroilna and their neighbors some of the advantages available to residents of the University. To this end, it offers (1) *Study Outlines* based on books of special interest, and (2) the loan of the recommended books to non-residents of Chapel Hill. To meet the growing demand for these privileges, the *Study Outlines* listed on the following pages of this booklet have been prepared by members of the University faculty and others connected with the University and its Library. These facilities are offered to clubs, libraries, discussion groups, correspondence and extension students, teachers and individual readers.

CLUBS, LIBRARIES, DISCUSSION AND STUDY GROUPS

By means of the *Study Outlines*, issued six times a year, assistance is given in the preparation of a year's study on a wide variety of subjects, such as poetry, art, music, drama, history, current fiction, biography, national and international problems, and current events. The reference material consists of books, magazines and pamphlets, the supply of which is constantly freshened by up-to-date material.

In addition, the Library maintains a separate collection of books of special interest to students and teachers, particularly those in correspondence and extension classes. This collection also includes plays, debates, and materials for essays and term papers.

It is not necessary, however, for an individual to be a member of a group or a student in school to obtain these privileges. The services and facilities of the University Library, through its Library Extension Department, are available to any citizen interested in cultural reading. Any book in the Library, not reserved for reference or class room use, may be lent by mail for a limited time. Also, through the Bull's Head Bookshop, which is a part of the Library Extension Department, recent fiction and new books of general interest may be borrowed on rental rates.

TERMS FOR REGISTERED CLUBS AND OTHER GROUPS

A registration fee of $7.00 is charged to clubs in North Carolina; $10.00 elsewhere. For this fee, ten copies of the selected *Study Outline* are supplied, and all necessary books for preparing papers are lent during the club year. There are usually twelve chapters in each *Study Outline*. Each chapter has an explanatory introduction, lists of books to be discussed, and suggestions for developing each topic. To these are appended a complete list of all books recommended and the addresses of publishers. There is also a skeleton outline of the entire course for convenience in assigning dates and leaders.

Books are sent two or three weeks in advance, and may be kept until the meeting has been held. Clubs are requested to submit their schedule when they register, so that the material for each date may be reserved. Clubs are requested also not to print their yearbooks, giving dates of programs, before the dates have been confirmed by this department, since occasionally it is necessary to change the order of chapters as given in the *Study Outlines*. This is not done, however, if there is a sequence of interest connecting the chapters, or if the rearrangement causes inconvenience to the clubs. Cooperation from the clubs is appreciated. The registration fee does not include transportation costs, which are payable by the borrower.

TERMS FOR NON-REGISTERED CLUBS AND OTHER BORROWERS

Non-registered clubs or members of non-registered clubs may borrow the books listed for a single topic in the *Study Outlines* for a fee of twenty-five cents, or all the books listed for one meeting for a fee of fifty cents.

Correspondence and extension students, teachers, pupils and general readers may borrow books on the following terms: For a fee of ten cents, one book may be borrowed for three weeks; for twenty-five cents, three books at one time for three weeks, provided they are not books previously reserved for club or local class-room use. New books not in the Library Extension collection may be borrowed through the Bull's Head Bookshop for twenty-five cents for two weeks. In all cases the borrower pays transportation costs both ways. Renewal fee is ten cents per week. Overdues, five cents per day. Always state if material is for club, school or general reading use.

Address all queries, requests, orders and suggestions to

Miss Nellie Roberson, *Head*
Library Extension Department
University Library
Chapel Hill, North Carolina

STUDY OUTLINES

VOLUME I

The Southern Garden. W. L. Hunt. October 1934. No. 1*
Adventures in Reading, Seventh Series. C. S. Love. January 1935. No. 2*
Below the Potomac. M. N. Bond. April 1935. No. 3*
Europe in Transition. Phillips Russell & C. M. Russell. May 1935. No. 4*
Other People's Lives, Fourth Series. C. S. Love. June 1935. No. 5*
The Story of Books. R. B. Downs. July 1935. No. 6*

VOLUME II

Adventures with Music and Musicians. A. D. McCall. October 1935. No. 1

Famous Women of Yesterday and Today. Revised Edition. C. S. Love.
  January 1936. No. 2*
Adventures in Reading, Eighth Series. M. N. Bond. April 1936. No. 3*
Other People's Lives, Fifth Series. C. S. Love. May 1936. No. 4
Adventures in Reading, Ninth Sereis. A. B. Adams. June 1936. No. 5
Modern Plays and Playwrights. C. M. Russell. July 1936. No. 6

VOLUME III

Adventures Around the World. Lucile Kelling. October 1936. No. 1*
The Modern Woman. E. C. Baity. January 1937. No. 2*
Literary Backgrounds of Present Day Germany. A. E. Zucker and W. P.
  Friederich. April 1937. No. 3
India in Revolution. E. E. and E. E. Ericson. May 1937. No. 4
Adventures in Reading, Tenth Series. A. B. Adams. June 1937. No. 5*
The Theatre Today. M. G. Holmes. July 1937. No. 6

VOLUME IV

Other People's Lives, Sixth Series. C. S. Love. October 1937. No. 1
American Humor. E. C. Downs & R. B. Downs. January 1938. No. 2
Contemporary Poetry. Lucile Kelling. April 1938. No. 3*
Building and Furnishing a Home. E. C. Baity. May 1938. No. 4
Adventures in Reading, Eleventh Series. A. B. Adams. June 1938. No. 5*
Famous Women of Yesterday and Today. Third Edition. C. S. Love. July
  1938. No. 6

VOLUME V

Political Problems in Present-Day Europe. First Series. Werner P. Fried-
  erich. October 1938. No. 1*
Political Problems in Present-Day Europe. Second Series. C. B. Robson,
  C. H. Pegg, A. B. Dugan, and J. L. Godfrey. January 1939. No. 2
Adventures in Reading, Twelfth Series. A. B. Adams. April 1939. No. 3*
The Modern Woman's Bookshelf. E. C. Baity. May 1939. No. 4
Adventures Around the World, Second Series. Lucile Kelling. June 1939.
  No. 5
At Home with the Fine Arts. M. G. Holmes. July 1939. No. 6*

VOLUME VI

The New Frontier. W. W. Drake. October 1939. No. 1
United States Mural; a Study of Regional Novels. Lucile Kelling. Janu-
  ary 1940. No. 2
Other People's Lives, Seventh Series. C. S. Love. April 1940. No. 3*
Adventures in Reading, Thirteenth Series. A. B. Adams. May 1940. No. 4
Adventures with Opera. A. D. McCall. June 1940. No. 5
Arts and Crafts in Georgian England. M. N. Bond. July 1940. No. 6

58 STUDY OUTLINES (Continued)

VOLUME VII

The United States in the World Crisis. E. S. & J. L. Godfrey. October 1940. No. 1
The Old North State. A. B. Adams. January 1941. No. 2
The Film Yesterday, Today and Tomorrow. Walter Spearman. April 1941. No. 3
Religion and Contemporary Life. Dale Spearman. May 1941. No. 4
"Eyes South." E. S. Godfrey and J. L. Godfrey. June 1941. No. 5
Adventures in Reading, Fourteenth Series. A. B. Adams. July 1941. No. 6

VOLUME VIII

The Modern Woman's Unfinished Business. E. C. Baity. October 1941. No. 1
Understanding the News. Walter Spearman. January 1942. No. 2
Adventures in Reading, Fifteenth Series. A. B. Adams. April 1942. No. 3
Other Peoples' Lives, Eighth Series. C. S. Love. May 1942. No. 4
Places and Peoples of the Pacific. D. & W. Spearman. June 1942. No. 5*
Blueprints for Tomorrow. A. B. Adams. July 1942. No. 6*

VOLUME IX

Some Leaders of the World at War. E. S. & J. L. Godfrey. October 1942. No. 1
Adventures in Reading, Sixteenth Series. D. & W. Spearman. January 1943. No. 2
The Homemaker Enlists. A. B. Adams. April 1943. No. 3
The Conflict of Political Ideas. L. O. Kattsoff. May 1943. No. 4
Adventures in Reading, Seventeenth Series. A. B. Adams. June 1943. No. 5
Places and Peoples of the Mediterranean. D. & W. Spearman. July 1943. No. 6

VOLUME X

Adventures in Reading, Eighteenth Series. A. B. Adams. January 1944. No. 1
Nature Writers in United States. A. B. Adams. April 1944. No. 2
Music in America. Adeline McCall. May 1944. No. 3
Other People's Lives, Ninth Series. C. S. Love. June 1944. No. 4
Blueprints for Tomorrow, Second Series. H. H. Robson. July 1944. No. 5
Adventures in Reading, Nineteenth Series. A. B. Adams. October 1944. No. 6

VOLUME XI

Contemporary Poetry, Second Series. Lucile Kelling. January 1945. No. 1
Gardens of the South. Elizabeth Lawrence. April 1945. No. 2
The Pacific World. Walter Spearman. May 1945. No. 3
A Journey to Mexico. Agatha B. Adams. June 1945. No. 4
The Pattern of America. Lucile Kelling. April 1946. No. 5
Women and the Wide World. E. Chesley Baity. May 1946. No. 6

Subscription per volume, $2.00; to residents of North Carolina, $1.00.
Single copies, 50 cents each; in North Carolina, 25 cents.

* Out of print. Available for lending only.

Studies in the History of N. C. 1923. R. D. W. Connor. Vol. III. No. 3
Present Day Literature. 1924. C. S. Love. Vol. III. No. 13
Great Composers, 1600-1900. 1925. Paul John Weaver. Vol. IV. No. 13
Good Books of 1924-1925. Cornelia S. Love. Vol. V. No. 3
A Study of Shakespeare. 1926. Russell Potter. Vol. V. No. 9
Studies in Southern Literature. Revised Edition. 1926. Addison Hibbard.
    Vol. V. No. 10
Current Books: 1925-1926. Cornelia Spencer Love. Vol. V. No. 14
A Study Course in International One-Act Plays. 1926. Ethel T. Rockwell.
    Vol. VI. No. 3
Studies in the Development of the Short Story: English and American. 1926.
    L. B. Wright. Vol. VI. No. 4
Studies in Modern Drama. Revised Edition. 1927. Elizabeth L. Green.
    Vol. VI. No. 9
Studies in American Literature. Revised Edition. 1927. Addison Hibbard.
    Vol. VI. No. 12
Modern French Art. 1927. Russell Potter. Vol. VI. No. 13
Adventures in Reading. 1927. Russell Potter. Vol. VII. No. 2
Our Heritage: A Study Through Literature of the American Tradition.
    1927. James Holly Hanford. Vol. VII. No. 4
The Negro in Contemporary American Literature. 1928. E. L. Green. Vol.
    VII. No. 14
Contemporary Southern Literature. 1928. Howard Mumford Jones. Vol.
    VIII. No. 3
Recent Poetry from the South. 1928. Addison Hibbard. Vol. VIII. No. 4
Contemporary Spanish Literature in English Translation. 1929. A. B. and
    N. B. Adams. Vol. VIII. No. 9
Adventures in Reading, Second Series. 1929. Russell Potter. Vol. VIII.
    No. 10
A Study of South America. 1929. W. W. Pierson & C. S. Love. Vol. VIII.
    No. 11
A Study of American Art and Southern Artists of Note. 1929. M. deB.
    Graves. Vol. IX. No. 2
A Study Course in American One-Act Plays. Revised Edition. 1929. E. T.
    Rockwell. Vol. IX. No. 3
Folklore. 1929. Ralph Steele Boggs. Vol. IX. No. 6
The French Novel in English Translation. 1930. U. T. Holmes, Jr. Vol.
    IX. No. 7
Art History. Mary deB. Graves. 1930. Vol. IX. No. 9
The South in Contemporary Literature. 1930. Addison Hibbard. Vol. IX.
    No. 10
Adventures in Reading, Third Series. 1930. Marjorie N. Bond and Rich-
    mond P. Bond. Vol. X. No. 1
Other People's Lives, Second Series. 1930. C. S. Love. Vol. X. No. 6
America and Her Music. 1931. Lamar Stringfield. Vol. X. No. 7
Studies in Confederate Leadership. 1931. F. M. Green. Vol. X. No. 8
Books of Travel. Revised Edition. 1931. U. T. Holmes, Jr. Vol. X. No. 10
Adventures in Reading, Fourth Series. 1931. Marjorie N. Bond and Rich-
    mond P. Bond. Vol. XI. No. 1
The Far East, with Special Reference to China. 1931. J. A. Robertson.
    Vol. XI. No. 2
Heroes of the American Revolution. 1931. F. M. Green. Vol. XI. No. 5
Romance of the Western Frontier. 1932. F. M. Green. Vol. XI. No. 8
Modern Russia. 1932. E. E. and E. E. Ericson. Vol. XII. No. 1
Twentieth Century American Literature. 1933. Revised Edition of *Con-
    temporary American Literature.* Marjorie N. Bond. Vol. XIII. No. 1
Other People's Lives, Third Series. 1933. C. S. Love. Vol. XIII. No. 2
Adventures in Reading, Sixth Series. 1933. M. N. Bond. Vol. XIII. No. 5

Single Copies, 50 cents; in North Carolina, 25 cents.

THE UNIVERSITY LIBRARY EXTENSION DEPARTMENT

CPSIA information can be obtained
at www.ICGtesting.com
Printed in the USA
BVHW091738021118
531990BV00019B/1012/P